The Island of Doctor Moreau

H.G. WELLS

Level 3

Retold by Fiona Beddall
Series Editors: Andy Hopkins and Jocelyn Potter

Pearson Education Limited
Edinburgh Gate, Harlow,
Essex CM20 2JE, England
and Associated Companies throughout the world.

ISBN: 978-1-4058-8190-6

First published 2007
This edition published 2008

Text copyright © Pearson Education Ltd 2008
Original text: © The Literary Executors of the Estate of H.G. Wells
Illustrations by David Kearney

1 3 5 7 9 10 8 6 4 2

Set in 11/14pt Bembo
Printed in China
SWTC/01

Published by Pearson Education Limited in association with
Penguin Books Ltd, both companies being subsidiaries of Pearson PLC

For a complete list of the titles available in the Penguin Readers series please write to your local
Pearson Longman office or to: Penguin Readers Marketing Department, Pearson Education,
Edinburgh Gate, Harlow, Essex CM20 2JE

Contents

		page
Introduction		v
Chapter 1	Lost and Found	1
Chapter 2	The *Ipecacuanha*	3
Chapter 3	Montgomery's island	6
Chapter 4	Dr Moreau	10
Chapter 5	An Evening Walk	13
Chapter 6	Moreau's Laboratory	16
Chapter 7	Meeting the Animal-men	18
Chapter 8	On the Beach	22
Chapter 9	Moreau's Work	26
Chapter 10	The Taste of Blood	28
Chapter 11	The Puma Escapes	33
Chapter 12	The Search for Moreau	36
Chapter 13	Montgomery's Party	39
Chapter 14	Alone with the Animal-men	43
Activities		48

Introduction

'Pain is just a little thing, Prendick. While you worry about pain, you are no better than an animal.'

Edward Prendick is travelling in the South Pacific when his ship goes down. He is saved after many days at sea by another ship; a passenger, Montgomery, nurses him back to health. Prendick becomes interested in the mystery of Montgomery's life. Why does he live on an unknown Pacific island? Who is his ugly assistant, with eyes that shine red in the dark? And why does he have a puma and other animals on board?

When the captain throws Prendick off the ship near Montgomery's island, he meets Montgomery's master, Doctor Moreau, a famous scientist with dark secrets. And he meets others on the island too – strange animal-like people who live in fear of Moreau, his laws and his House of Pain.

Herbert George Wells was born near London in 1866. His father was a shopkeeper and a professional sportsman. But his sporting life ended suddenly when he broke his leg. Soon his business failed too, and his family became very poor. At the age of thirteen, young Herbert had to get a job.

For two years he was a shop assistant. He worked thirteen-hour days and slept with the other assistants in a room above the shop. He was very unhappy. Finally he found a better job, as an assistant teacher near his mother's new home in Sussex. He was able to study in the evenings. After excellent results in some science examinations, he won a free place at the famous Normal School of Science in London.

At first he studied hard. He was taught by T. H. Huxley, an important biologist and a close friend of Charles Darwin. Wells never forgot Huxley's lessons, but he had few good memories of his other teachers. He found laboratory work slow and boring, and he soon lost interest in his studies. He spent most of his time reading history and literature. He also started a student magazine. He failed his final science examinations.

While he worked as a school science teacher, he returned to his own studies. At the age of twenty-four he finally passed his university examinations in biology and became a university teacher. He also became a writer around this time. He wrote both serious pieces and funny short stories for newspapers and magazines. His first book was for students of biology.

In 1893, he became very ill. He had to give up his job at the university. Luckily, he was starting to make enough money from his work as a writer.

His first fiction book was *The Time Machine* (1895). It was an immediate success and other books soon followed: *The Island of Doctor Moreau* (1896), *The Invisible Man* (1897), *The War of the Worlds* (1898). (These four books are all Penguin Readers.) Wells's work was a new form of literature, mixing adventure stories with more serious messages about the future of Man and Man's position in the world. By 1900, Wells was even more popular than Jules Verne, a writer of similar science fiction stories in French.

But Wells wanted to be famous for more than adventure stories. He wrote many works of real-world fiction. These were very successful at the time but are not often read now. He also wrote serious books asking for a fairer Britain and better lives for the poor and for women. He was an internationally famous thinker, and his voice was often heard on the radio. In 1920 he met Lenin in Russia, and in 1934 he visited Roosevelt in the United States and Stalin in Russia.

In total he wrote more than 150 books, fifty of them works of fiction. He died in 1946.

In the early 1800s, most people in Britain believed the story of Adam and Eve.* They believed that God, the father of the world, made Man in his own shape. People thought that the natural world was kind and good.

But, in 1856, Charles Darwin changed everything. He wrote that man is a relative of the ape. As this idea was slowly accepted, people felt differently about the natural world. Nothing was planned. Nothing was for ever. We were no different from other animals in the past, but we changed. Perhaps, one day, we will change again. Will we get cleverer? Or will we change back to the animals that we were? These questions are at the heart of *The Island of Doctor Moreau*.

People's ideas about God changed too. Science could explain the world without God. Religion seemed unnecessary. For some, it was bad, dangerous. White-haired old Doctor Moreau in Wells's story is like God. But he is a bad God, an unkind God ... and his work destroys him.

Wells was writing when Britain ruled large parts of Asia, Africa and the Caribbean. There were already problems between the British and the local people. These problems grew more serious, and British rule ended in most places after the Second World War. Wells understood these problems very clearly. At first, the dark-skinned people on Moreau's island work for their Master and follow the Law. But, as in the real world of Wells's future, this unnatural rule is soon thrown out.

Wells's strange story of Moreau's island is hard to forget. And its main message is still important today. Science can make new lives and it can change lives. But we must not experiment with life just because we can. Without a strong reason for a scientific experiment, the results can be truly terrible.

*Adam and Eve: the first man and woman in the books of the Christian, Jewish and Muslim religions

In my weak state, I lay in the boat, laughing quietly.

Chapter 1 Lost and Found

I was one of the few lucky passengers on the *Lady Vain*. When the ship went down in the Pacific in February 1887, I found myself in a small boat with another passenger, Helmar, and a sailor. I never knew the sailor's name. A fourth man jumped from the ship, trying to reach us. But his head hit the side of the ship. He went down under the water and never came up again.

We had only a little bread and a small container of water on board. On the first day, the sea was very rough and we were almost thrown out of the boat. But then the sea became calmer and that danger passed. We spoke little. Most of the time, we did not move. We lay under the hot sun, looking out across the ocean.

On the fourth day, we had no more water to drink. We became very thirsty. Then on the sixth day, Helmar finally spoke of the idea that was already in all our minds. 'We need to kill someone. Then the other two can drink his blood.'

Helmar had two longer sticks and one shorter one. The person with the short stick had to die. But the sailor chose the short stick and he did not accept the result. The love of life was too strong in him. He attacked Helmar, and the two men fought. I tried to help Helmar. But as I was going towards them, the boat moved suddenly. Helmar and the sailor fell straight over the side together and went down like stones.

In my weak state, I lay in the boat, laughing quietly. I did not know why I was laughing. But for many minutes I could not stop.

After that, I did nothing. I thought about drinking sea water. That way I could die more quickly. But I was too weak even for this.

On the eighth day, I saw a sail far away across the sea. I remember thinking, 'How strange. A ship is coming, but too late, because I'm already dead.' Hour after hour, I lay with my head on the side of the boat, and the sail came closer and closer. I did nothing to call the ship to me. But still it came. I remember seeing the side of the ship next to my boat, and then … nothing.

I woke in a small, untidy room on board the ship. A young man was sitting by my bed, holding my wrist. He had fair hair, a thick moustache and grey, watery eyes.

The man started speaking. Suddenly, from above us, came the sound of metal against metal and then the low, angry growl of an animal.

The man showed no surprise, but repeated his question: 'How do you feel now?'

I tried to speak, but no sound came from my mouth. Luckily the man saw the question in my eyes.

'You were found in a small boat. You had no food or drink.'

I looked at my hand – terribly thin, with the skin hanging off it. Suddenly, I remembered my long days lost at sea.

'Have some of this,' said the man, offering me a red drink.

It tasted like blood, but I drank it all. I soon felt a bit stronger.

'You are lucky that I know about medicine,' said the man.

'What ship is this?' I asked slowly and painfully. These were my first words for many days.

'The *Ipecacuanha*. Oh, and I'm Montgomery.'

The noise above us began again.

'You'll be OK now,' continued Montgomery. 'You've been asleep for almost thirty hours, you know.'

I heard a number of dogs up above.

'Can I eat?' I asked.

'Of course. The cook is already preparing a meal for you.'

'That sounds wonderful,' I replied.

'But tell me, what happened to you? Why were you alone in that boat? … *Damn that noise!*' He stood up suddenly and left the room. He shouted at someone for a minute, then returned.

2

'Well, you were starting to tell me your story,' he said.

I told him my name, Edward Prendick. I was, I said, travelling in the Pacific because of my interest in natural history. He was excited by this, and told me about his own days as a biology student in London. He asked me many questions about his favourite places in the city – the university, the shops and, most of all, the clubs.

'They were happy days,' he said sadly. 'But then I did something silly, and it all ended suddenly. Ten years ago now … I'll just go and ask the cook about your food.'

The growls above us started again, even louder and angrier.

'What's that?' I called after him, but the door was already closing. Montgomery came back a minute later with some food, and in my excitement at the wonderful smell I forgot about the animal noises.

Chapter 2   The *Ipecacuanha*

I spent the day either eating or sleeping. The next morning I felt stronger and got out of bed. Montgomery lent me some clothes. They were too big – Montgomery was a tall man. But since my own clothes were destroyed, I was very grateful to him.

As I dressed, he told me about the *Ipecacuanha*'s captain, Davis. 'He's drunk most of the time. But I don't have to worry about him for much longer. I'm getting off the ship soon.'

'Where?' I asked, surprised. Were we not still in the middle of the Pacific Ocean?

'At the island where I live. I don't think it has a name.'

He gave me a hard look. 'No more questions,' his eyes seemed to say. Then I followed him out of the room for a walk around the ship.

On the ladder to the top part of the ship, there was a man in our way. I could only see the man's back, but even from this view he seemed strange. He was very short and wide, with a hairy neck and a head that was in front of, not above, his shoulders. He wore dark blue work clothes and had long, thick black hair.

The man heard our steps and looked round with the speed of an animal. His face was even stranger than his body. He had black skin and dark eyes with almost no white in them. His mouth was shaped more like a bear's or a dog's than a man's, with the largest teeth that you can imagine. The ugliness of this man hit me like a wave, and in my weak state I almost fell. But Montgomery held my arm and helped me towards the ladder.

'Get out of our way, M'ling!' he shouted at the man. 'You shouldn't be here. Your place is at the front of the ship, with the sailors.'

'They don't want me with them,' replied the man called M'ling.

'They don't want you with them? Don't be so stupid. Go, I say!'

M'ling moved away slowly, and I followed Montgomery up the ladder. At the top I discovered where all the animal noises were coming from. There were lots of dogs tied up in one corner. In another corner was a puma in a cage that was too small for it. Rabbits, also in cages, filled the rest of the space. There were bits of animal food everywhere, and the smell was terrible.

Suddenly there was a cry from the front of the ship, and someone shouted angrily. The strange man with the black face, M'ling, ran towards us, followed by a man with red hair and a white hat. When the dogs saw M'ling, they became even noisier than before. He stopped near them for a second. The other man reached him and hit him hard between the shoulders. M'ling fell down next to the dogs, crying out in pain. The dogs growled angrily and jumped on him. Some sailors came to watch with interest. They did not try to help.

'Stop that!' shouted Montgomery, hurrying towards them.

M'ling finally pushed the dogs away and stood up. He held on to the side of the ship, clearly afraid of the red-haired man's next move.

Montgomery reached them. 'This must stop, Captain,' he said angrily, holding on to the red-haired man's arm.

I stood behind Montgomery. The captain turned and looked at us rudely. His body moved from side to side as he stood there. He was clearly drunk.

'What must stop?' he laughed.

'M'ling is your passenger. Keep your hands off him or ...'

'Damn you, Montgomery! This is my ship, and I make the rules!'

'M'ling works for me. Don't hurt him again, do you hear?'

The captain looked at Montgomery sleepily for about a minute. 'Damn scientists,' he finally said in reply.

Montgomery was getting very angry.

'He's drunk, Montgomery,' I said to him. 'He won't listen when he's like this.'

'He's always drunk,' Montgomery answered. 'Does that give him permission to hit his passengers?'

'My ship,' the captain said, waving his hand at the cages, 'was a clean ship. Look at it now!'

'You agreed to take the animals,' shouted Montgomery.

'And why do you want animals like these on your damn island, hey? And that man of yours! He's not a man. He's a monster!'

'You leave him alone, I say,' continued Montgomery.

'I'll cut out his insides if he comes to the front of the ship again. Sailors only at the front. Cut out his damn insides, I will! Damn you, and damn your crazy island ...'

The captain continued to shout at Montgomery for some time. Montgomery took a step towards him. I did not want a fight on board, so I stopped him.

'He's drunk,' I said. 'Just leave him.'

The captain started shouting rudely again.

'That's enough!' I shouted back at him.

It was not sensible to shout at the captain, of course. I was alive only as a result of his help. And I had no money to pay for my journey on his ship.

For some time he shouted angrily about his kindness to me. But there was no fight between Montgomery and the captain, and for that I was grateful.

Chapter 3   Montgomery's Island

Late that evening, we saw land far out to sea and the ship turned towards it. We were nearing Montgomery's island.

After supper, Montgomery and I stood outside, talking under the stars. I was interested to know more about his animals and his island home. But he seemed uncomfortable with my questions, so I soon changed the subject. We spoke about London, and about science. But as we talked, my questions grew stronger in my mind. Why was a man of science living on an unknown island in the middle of the Pacific? Why was he taking the puma, rabbits and dogs there? And who was that strange man who worked for him?

I heard a noise behind me and turned. Montgomery's dark assistant was standing a few steps from us. He looked quickly towards me. For a second or two, his eyes shone red in the lights of the ship. It frightened me terribly. I thought of the stories that I read as a child, of monsters and strange animals of the night. Then the man looked away, and Montgomery was saying, 'I'm going to bed now. There'll be lots to do in the morning.'

I followed him down the ladder and went to my room. I slept little that night. I was woken many times, both by the noises of the dogs and by my terrible dreams.

Early the next morning, I woke to a new sound. Someone above me was pushing the animal cages across the ship. I climbed the ladder. At the top, six men were carrying the puma in his cage to the side of the ship. A large man with white hair was now on board, talking to Montgomery. Next to them was a ladder down to a small boat that was waiting below. The captain, Davis, was there too. 'We'll soon have a clean ship again,' he was shouting. It was clear that he was still drunk.

When the captain saw me, his rudeness from the night before began again. This was no surprise to me, but I never for a second imagined his next move. Pointing to the ladder down the side of the ship, Davis shouted, 'That way! That way, Mr No-Money!'

'I don't understand,' I said. 'What do you mean?'

'I mean that we're cleaning out the ship. No room for Mr No-Money. It's time for you to go. That way, I say! That way!'

I looked at the captain in surprise. It was clear from his face that this was not a joke. But I was not too worried. The idea of a journey across the ocean with the drunk captain and his unfriendly sailors was not much fun. And I wanted to find out more about Montgomery and his mysterious island.

I turned to Montgomery. But the white-haired man next to him said quickly, 'We can't have you.'

'You can't have me?' I asked, very worried now. 'Well, Captain …' I began.

He stopped me. 'That way now, Mr No-Money. If they don't want you, we'll put you back in your boat. The boat from the *Lady Vain*. You can't stay with us. Go, I say!'

'But Montgomery!' I cried.

He shook his head and looked quickly at the man with white hair. 'He's the boss. I can't help you,' he seemed to say.

I looked from the captain to Montgomery to the man with white hair. I cried to each man to help me. But none of them listened.

When all of Montgomery's things were in his master's boat, it moved away from our ship towards a beach on the island, with Montgomery, his master and M'ling on board. The sailors then threw me roughly into the little boat where my troubles began twelve days before. It was half full of water and had no food or drink on board. They pushed the boat out to sea. I lay in the water at the bottom of it, crying like a baby.

Luckily, Montgomery's master saw me in my boat and changed his mind. He turned his boat round to help me. I stopped crying, but my need was urgent. With so much water on board, my boat was going down fast.

They had no space for me. There were three men from the island in their boat, with Montgomery, his master, M'ling and all the animals and boxes from the *Ipecacuanha*. But I used a cup from their boat to get out the water in the bottom of mine. Then we tied the two boats together and they pulled me slowly to land.

As we travelled in this way, I looked more carefully at the people in the boat. I now saw that Montgomery's master, the white-haired man, was quite old – sixty or more. I remembered from the *Ipecacuanha* that he was a very tall man. But as he sat next to the other three men from the island, his head only reached their shoulders. Were the men of this island the tallest in the world?

Their height was not the only unusual thing about them. They had long, straight, black hair like the hair on a horse's neck, and they were covered from head to foot in dirty white cotton. Under the cotton, I could see dark, strangely-shaped faces with bright eyes and big teeth. As I looked at them, I started to feel ill. I quickly looked away.

We were nearing the island. There was a beach of grey sand, with tall trees behind it. Between the trees was a simple house circled by a big stone wall.

Soon we landed on the beach. The three men in white cotton helped Montgomery to carry the boxes onto the sand. I realised then that they were not very tall. But their bodies were unusually long, and the top part of their legs very short. Their knees moved in a very strange way when they walked. As the white-haired man passed them with the dogs, the dogs growled angrily at them.

Then we tied the two boats together and they pulled me slowly to land.

I smiled gratefully as Montgomery's master came towards me. 'Montgomery says that you're a man of science,' he said. 'We're scientists here, too, you know – biologists … You'll probably be with us for twelve months or more. Ships don't pass this island very often.'

Chapter 4   Dr Moreau

The white-haired man turned and walked quickly towards the house up the hill. I went to talk to Montgomery.

'You've saved me again,' I said gratefully.

'Well, this island's not exactly London,' he replied. 'I can't promise that you'll enjoy yourself here. You'll have to be careful with …' He stopped suddenly. 'Can you help me with these rabbits?'

He carried a cage of rabbits from the boat to the beach, opened the cage door and threw the rabbits onto the sand. 'Go and have lots of babies!' he said as they ran towards the trees. 'There isn't much meat to eat on the island,' he explained to me. 'We're hoping that the rabbits will make good food.'

I helped Montgomery with the rabbits until the white-haired man returned. Then the three of us walked together to the stone wall that circled the house.

'Well, Montgomery, what are we going to do with him?' the white-haired man asked. 'He can't come into the house, but he can't stay out here either. We don't have time to build him a new house.'

'He should have my room,' answered Montgomery. 'He can use the outside door.'

The white-haired man opened an outside door with a heavy key and we all went inside. There was another door on the far side of the room, into the garden behind the stone wall. The door was half open. Montgomery quickly crossed the room and locked the door.

'Keep that door closed at all times,' his master said to me. 'We don't want any accidents.' He gave Montgomery a strange look. 'And we must get you some food,' he continued. 'We didn't invite you here, of course, but you're our guest now. We'll try to make you comfortable.' Then he walked out of the room by the outside door.

The room was small but pleasant. There was a little bed, a table and chair, and some books about medicine.

'We usually have our meals in here,' said Montgomery. Then he followed his master outside. 'Moreau!' he shouted. 'Moreau!'

'Moreau,' I thought. 'Where have I heard that name before?'

Montgomery's assistant, M'ling, came into the room, bringing some coffee, a plate of vegetables and a bottle of whisky. As he put the food on the table, his long hair fell in front of his face. I saw one of his ears. It had a sharp point at the top and was covered in thick hair!

'Your breakfast, Mr Prendick,' he said as he left the room. I started to eat the food gratefully. But I left the whisky – I have never been a drinker.

Suddenly, I remembered! Moreau! He was in all the papers, eight, maybe ten years before. An important biologist – a very successful man. But then a newspaper sent someone to work as his assistant. There were terrible stories about the animals that he used in his experiments. A dog escaped from his laboratory without any skin on its body. Other animals were found there in terrible pain. The newspapers attacked Moreau and his work, and no one in the scientific world defended him. He had to close his laboratory.

I was sure that this was the same man. Perhaps it was too hard for Moreau to stop his work. Perhaps he chose to continue it on an island far from home.

This idea explained the puma and the other animals from the *Ipecacuanha*. But why were Moreau and Montgomery trying to keep everything secret from me? Laboratory work on animals was not very pleasant, but to a man of science like me it was not so terrible. Was there something more? Something about M'ling and those other strange men on the island? My mind filled with possible explanations, each one more terrible than the last.

At about one o'clock, Montgomery came into the room. M'ling was following him, carrying our lunch – some bread, a bowl of salad, a bottle of whisky and some water.

'Moreau isn't stopping for lunch today,' said Montgomery. 'He's too busy with his work.'

'Moreau,' I said. 'I know that name.'

'Damn! Do you? Well, you'll understand something about the "mysteries" in the laboratory then. Whisky?'

'No thanks,' I replied. 'I don't drink.'

'Very sensible! It was drink that brought me here. I drank too much and did something silly. Moreau offered his help and … How stupid I was!'

'Montgomery,' I said suddenly, 'why has M'ling got strangely-shaped ears?'

'Er, M'ling? But … er … his hair covers his ears. How do you know about his ears?'

'I've seen them, Montgomery. They've got a sharp point at the top. And his eyes shine in the dark.'

'Well, er … I don't know, Prendick. I've never seen his ears. Maybe he keeps his hair long to hide them.'

From the laboratory we heard a loud cry of pain. It sounded like the puma. The noise continued for about a minute, and it clearly troubled Montgomery. 'Damn, damn, damn,' he was saying quietly to himself. He drank a big glass of whisky, then left the room.

Chapter 5   An Evening Walk

Through the afternoon, it seemed that the puma's pain got worse. The screams grew louder and louder. I put my fingers in my ears, but still the screams filled my head. Finally I had to escape from the room. I went outside, but the noise from the laboratory was even louder there. I walked quickly away from the house and into the forest, until I could not hear the puma any more. At last I felt calmer.

I came to a stream. It was a pleasant place, protected from the hot afternoon sun by the tall trees above. I sat down to rest. Suddenly, I saw something moving in the shadows on the other side of the stream. It came closer. What was it?

It moved towards the stream. It was an animal, coming for a drink. It drank thirstily, with its head down at the water. I looked more carefully. It was not an animal! It was a man, dressed in blue clothes. But this man was using his hands as feet, and he was drinking like a cat!

I moved to see him better. He heard me and looked up. Our eyes met. He stood up quickly and dried his mouth with his hand. His legs were much shorter than his body. He looked at me for a minute, then walked slowly away.

I too started walking. I did not feel comfortable by the stream now. I crossed it and went uphill. I was surprised by a bright red piece of ground, in the middle of the green of the plants. I looked closer. There was a dead rabbit there, half eaten and still warm. I thought about its killer – a dangerous animal or … that strange man by the stream? I realised that I knew nothing about the dangers of the animals or people in the forest. It was a bad idea to walk alone in a strange place like this. I decided to go back to the house.

I started running. I almost ran straight out into an open space, but stopped myself just in time. In this space between the trees, I

This man was using his hands as feet, and he was drinking like a cat!

saw three strange people. One was clearly female, the other two male. They had rough pink skin, and small bits of red clothes tied around their bodies. Their faces were heavy and shapeless, and they had almost no hair on their heads. Their legs were unusually short, and their feet were very small, with no toes. They talked quietly together – or were they singing? They moved their bodies from side to side in a kind of dance, and repeated the same words again and again. Memories of Sundays in church came back to me. Were these strange people practising their religion?

I continued to watch them. There was something animal about these people. At first this idea was not clear in my mind. But then one of the men fell to the ground. For a few seconds he was using his arms as legs, and suddenly I realised. With their rough pink skin and heavy faces, these people were like pigs!

I moved away from them as quietly as possible and walked towards the beach. Suddenly, thirty metres in front of me, I saw the man who was drinking at the stream earlier. His eyes shone green as he looked at me. Then he disappeared between the trees. I did not move. I could still feel his eyes on me.

'Who are you?' I shouted. But there was no answer, and I could see nothing in the shadows of the forest.

I realised now that it was getting dark. I needed to reach the house quickly. The idea of a night alone in the middle of the forest was too terrible to think about.

I started walking again. I felt that someone was following me. But each time I looked back, I saw nothing. For a long time I could not find the beach. I went one way, then another, losing hope. But finally I heard the sea. I followed the sound, and after a few minutes the forest opened onto the beach. Gratefully, I started walking along the sand.

When I stopped for a rest, a shadow behind me stopped too. 'Who's there?' I asked shakily. The thing did not reply. As I stepped back, my foot hit a stone. With my eyes still on the shadow, I slowly picked it up. Seeing my movement, the thing moved away.

Crazy with fear, I now ran. I heard feet behind me, and I ran faster. The yellow light from the house was in front of me, but still far away, too far. The thing behind me was getting closer and closer. It jumped at me, and I turned towards it with the stone in my hand. The stone hit its head, and it fell down onto the sand.

Chapter 6   Moreau's Laboratory

Shaking, I ran towards the house. I heard Montgomery's voice. 'Prendick?' he was shouting. 'Prendick!'

When I reached him, I fell weakly into his arms.

'Where have you been?' he asked. 'We were working all afternoon and we forgot about you. We only started looking half an hour ago.'

He helped me into the house, and I sat down. I was still shaking terribly.

'A walk in the dark, alone! What were you thinking, Prendick? I was afraid that ...'

'Please!' I said quickly. 'Please, lock that door!'

He looked at me carefully. 'So you've met some of our ... people.' He locked the door and gave me some whisky. For the first time in my life, I drank it.

I described the attack on the beach, and the strange people in the forest. 'What does it all mean, Montgomery?' I asked.

'It's nothing too terrible, I promise you,' he replied. 'But you've had enough for one day. You should get some sleep.'

'But what was that thing on the beach? Was it an animal, or was it a man?'

'Listen, Prendick. You've had a terrible few days, and you haven't had enough sleep. Drink this medicine so you can sleep through the noise of that damn puma. We'll talk in the morning.'

He was right. I was too tired to talk now. I drank his medicine. He helped me into bed like a child, and soon I was asleep.

When I woke, it was late morning. There was some breakfast on the table, and I ate hungrily. Montgomery opened the inside door – the door into the garden – for a quick hello. 'We're very busy in here, I'm afraid. No time to talk.' He closed the door again. But I discovered later that he did not lock it.

I returned to my breakfast. Suddenly there was a cry of pain from the laboratory. But this time it was not the puma. It sounded exactly like the cry of a man.

I did not move. My ears waited for the sound again, but there was nothing. 'Perhaps it was my imagination,' I thought.

Then it came again. This time there could be no mistake. A man in the laboratory was screaming and crying with pain. I ran straight to the door to the garden, threw it open and went outside.

Montgomery was near the door. 'Prendick, stop!' he shouted. Through an open door on the far side of the garden, I saw something pink, tied to a table. It was covered in blood and bits of white cloth. Then Moreau was in front of me. He picked me up and threw me back into my room. I heard the key in the lock, and Moreau saying, 'I'm not going to stop the work of a lifetime because of him.'

'But he doesn't understand,' said Montgomery.

I could not hear the rest. As I stood up shakily, my mind was full of the most terrible ideas. What were they doing to the man in there? I thought again about those strange people in the forest. Were they the results of Moreau's terrible experiments on ordinary men and women? It seemed the most believable explanation. And what about me? Did they plan to use me in their experiments too? It was clear to me that my life was in very great danger.

Luckily the outside door was still open. I picked up a walking stick to defend myself against these crazy scientists. Then I ran to the door.

I heard someone outside. It was Montgomery. Was he planning to lock me in my room? I ran at him with my stick, and he stepped back. 'Prendick!' he cried out in surprise. 'Don't be stupid, man!'

I ran north along the beach. Montgomery was behind me, shouting. I could not hear his words. I turned into the forest and ran for a kilometre or two. Then I stopped and listened. I heard a dog, then Montgomery's voice, but they were getting further and further away. No one was following me. I found a good place to hide, in the shadows of the trees. There I sat for many hours, too afraid to move.

I tried to make a plan. But how could I live alone on the island? I did not know how to catch rabbits or fish without the right equipment. I did not know what forest fruits and vegetables to eat. Could I ask the strange animal-men of the island for help? How dangerous were they?

My hiding place was getting uncomfortable, so I lay on the ground for a minute. Suddenly, high above me in the trees, I saw a pair of eyes … a black face … The face moved closer. I held my stick tightly as an ape-like person dropped from the trees.

'You, you, you,' he said.

Chapter 7   Meeting the Animal-men

'You,' he said again. 'In the boat.'

'Yes,' I answered. 'I came in the boat. From the ship.'

'Oh!' he said. His eyes travelled over me – my legs, my body, my face, my hands, the stick that I was carrying. His eyes returned to my hands. He held out his own hand and counted his fingers. 'One, two, three, four, five, eh?'

I guessed that he was counting his fingers as a way to greet me. I did the same. 'One, two, three, four, five, eh?' I said.

He gave me a wide smile, then disappeared into the trees. I tried to follow. I found him hanging on to a tree by one arm.

'Excuse me,' I said.

He dropped to the ground. Standing up straight, his arms hung below his knees.

'Do you know where to find food?' I continued.

'Food!' he said. 'Eat man's food now! At the huts!'

'But where are the huts?' I asked. 'I'm new here, you see.'

Together we walked through the forest. I wanted to find out as much as possible from him.

'How long have you been here?' I asked.

'How long?' he repeated.

When I asked my question again, he held up three fingers. Did he mean three months? Three years? I was not sure. I tried some other questions. His answers were difficult to understand. Some were on a completely different subject. After Moreau's experiments on him, this man was unable to have a sensible conversation.

After a long walk, we came to a rocky place near the sea. I followed the ape-man along a narrow path between two rocks. It went downhill steeply, getting darker and darker. At the bottom, in complete darkness, the ape-man stopped and said, 'Home.'

The place had a terrible smell, and there were strange noises all around me. Slowly my eyes started to see. I was standing next to a line of huts that used the steep rock face for their back walls, and bits of tree for their front walls and roofs. There was old fruit everywhere, and some simple cups made of wood. Strange people, large and small and of different shapes were hiding in the shadows.

My ape-man went into one of the huts. I held on tightly to my stick and followed him inside.

In the far corner of the hut sat a big, shapeless thing. The hut was too dark to see the thing's face.

The ape-man started talking to it. 'Look! It's a man! A man! A man, like me!'

'It's a man,' agreed the thing in the corner. 'Is he going to live with us?'

'Yes,' I said.

'Then he must learn the Law.'

Other people were coming into the hut now. There was quite a crowd.

'Say the words,' said the thing in the corner. '"Don't go on four legs. That is the Law. Are we not men?"'

I did not know what to do.

'Say the words,' said the ape-man.

'Say the words,' said the rest of the crowd angrily.

At last I understood them and repeated the words. The others repeated them after me, and soon we were all moving from side to side in the strangest way. This was clearly their religion. I was not in a position to question it.

'Don't go on four legs. That is the Law. Are we not men?' we repeated.

'Don't drink without cups. That is the Law. Are we not men?

'Don't eat meat or fish. That is the Law. Are we not men?

'Don't fight with heads or teeth. That is the Law. Are we not men?

'Don't run after other people. That is the Law. Are we not men?'

Then the words changed.

'His house is the House of Pain.

'His hands are the Hands that hurt.

'His hands are the Hands that make.

'His hands are the Hands that mend.

'He is Master of the stars in the sky.

'He is Master of the sun and moon.

'He is Master of the deep salt sea.

'He is our Master.'

At last the strange words ended. My eyes were now seeing better in the dark. The speaker in the corner was about the height and weight of an ordinary man, but was covered from head to foot in grey hair, like a big grey dog. What was he? What were they all?

'He's a five-man, a five-man like me,' said the ape-man.

The thing in the corner moved to the light of the hut's entrance and took my hand in his. His hand was hard, with three very short, thick fingers.

'Five fingers. Five thin fingers. That's good. Many have problems with their fingers.' He dropped my hand and looked into my eyes.

'I am the Sayer of the Law,' he said. 'New people come to me to learn the Law. Do not break the Law. No one escapes.'

'No one escapes,' repeated the animal-people.

'No one, no one,' said the ape-man. 'Once I did a little thing, a wrong thing. And look! He burned my hand. There! You can see the burn. The Master is great. The Master is good.'

'Different parts of the Law are difficult for different people,' explained the Sayer of the Law. 'Some like to bite and drink blood. Others like to fight with their heads or their hands. Others like to move the earth with their noses in the ground. These things are bad.'

'No one escapes,' said the men at the door.

'Punishment is quick and terrible,' continued the Sayer of the Law. 'So learn the Law. Say the words.' He began again from the start.

'Don't go on four legs. That is the Law. Are we not men?'

We were all making a lot of noise as we repeated the strange words. Because of this, I did not notice the growls of the dogs outside. But suddenly one of the pig-men put his head round the door and spoke urgently to the others. Everyone hurried out of the hut and I was left alone. Too late, I heard the dogs. As I reached the hut's entrance, Moreau, Montgomery and the

21

dogs were coming down the steep path between the rocks. Montgomery was pointing his gun at me.

Chapter 8   On the Beach

I held my stick tightly and looked around. There was a narrow space between the rocks. I ran towards it.

'Hold him!' shouted Moreau.

The animal-people moved towards me. I pushed into one man's shoulder and he fell against one of his friends. I used my stick on a third as he tried to catch my legs. Then I ran as fast as I could, up between the rocks and into the forest.

I could hear cries of 'Catch him! Hold him!' behind me. But luckily the animal-man nearest me was too wide for the narrow space between the rocks, and the others could not get past him for a minute or two. I went deeper into the forest, cutting my legs on the plants. Soon they were following me, crying like hungry and excited animals.

I ran and ran. They were getting closer. Finally, shaking with fear, I turned sharply to the right. The noises of my followers grew quieter as they continued straight on. For a short time I was safe.

But I knew now that the animal-people were as dangerous as Moreau and Montgomery. I could not ask them for protection. I decided to go back to the house. Maybe I could find a gun or knife there. It was my only hope.

I walked along the beach, leaving behind me a thin line of blood from my leg. Suddenly, far in front of me, Moreau, Montgomery and the dogs came out of the trees, with the animal-people close behind them. As they came towards me, I had no more hope of life. But I could still choose something better than the pain of Moreau's laboratory. I walked straight into the sea.

'Hold him!' shouted Moreau.

When I was thirty metres out, the water was still only at my waist. From the beach, Montgomery shouted, 'What are you doing, man?'

'I'm going to kill myself,' I said.

Montgomery looked at Moreau. 'Why?' Moreau asked.

'Because it's better to be dead than one of your experiments.'

'I told you,' Montgomery said to Moreau.

'Why do you think that you'll be one of my experiments?' asked Moreau.

'I saw him ... in your laboratory. And those animal-people. They ...'

'Stop!' said Moreau. The animal-men were listening to us from the tree-line.

'I won't stop!' I cried. 'Those poor people. They were men. But you've changed them. You've turned them into animals ... monsters!'

Montgomery looked very worried. 'Stop that, Prendick! Please, man, stop!'

The animal-people looked at me strangely. They moved closer to hear me better.

'Listen to me for a minute,' said Moreau. 'But in Latin.* I hope you learnt it at school.' He started speaking to me in Latin. My Latin was not very good, but his meaning was clear. These animal-people were not men, he explained. They were ordinary animals until he changed them in his laboratory.

'I don't believe you,' I replied in English. 'They talk. They build houses. They use tools. Animals can't do these things.'

'Come back to the house and I'll explain,' he called.

'No, I'm staying here.'

'The sea here is full of dangerous fish. They'll eat you if you go much further.'

*Latin: the language of the people of Rome about two thousand years ago and used in later years as the international language of science

'That's fine,' I answered. 'Better than your laboratory.'

'Wait a minute,' he said. He took a gun out of his pocket and put it down on the sand. 'Montgomery will do the same,' he said. 'We'll go up to the top of the beach. Then you can get the guns.'

'I won't,' I answered. 'You've probably got a third gun somewhere.'

'Think sensibly, Prendick. We didn't want to have you on this island. Why not, if we needed you for our experiments?'

'Why did you tell the animal-people to catch me?' I asked.

'This island is dangerous. We wanted to bring you back to the house. It's safer there.'

I was silent, thinking. Was it possible that his words were true?

'But I saw,' I said, 'in the laboratory …'

'That was the puma!' cried Montgomery. 'Listen, Prendick, this is crazy. Come out of the water, pick up the guns and talk.'

I was still afraid of Moreau, but Montgomery seemed an ordinary, honest kind of man. I decided to believe their story.

'Go up the beach, with your hands above your heads,' I said.

'We can't do that,' said Montgomery, moving his eyes towards the animal-people. 'They mustn't see their masters in a position of weakness.'

'Well, OK. But go back as far as the trees.'

When Moreau and Montgomery were at the tree-line, I picked up the guns and joined them under the trees.

'That's better,' said Moreau in an unfriendly voice. 'I've lost a day's work because of you.' Without another word, he and Montgomery turned and walked back towards the house.

The animal-people watched me silently. Were they ordinary animals in the past? Perhaps. But in that minute they had the look of small children. Small children who were trying to think.

Chapter 9   Moreau's Work

'You really are an impossible guest,' said Moreau after supper. 'If you try to kill yourself again, I won't stop you.'

He sat at the table, smoking. I sat as far away from him as possible, with the two guns still in my hands. Montgomery was not there. I did not feel comfortable yet with both of them in this small room with me.

'So, Prendick,' said Moreau, 'I've shown you the puma in the laboratory. Do you agree that it's a puma, not a man?'

'Yes, it's a puma. But you've done terrible things to it. I hope I never see an animal hurt like that again. You ...'

'Stop, Prendick, stop. Montgomery spoke like that when he was first here. It's really very boring. Right, you agree that it's the puma. Now be quiet so I can give you a lesson in biology.

'It's surprising that no one has done my kind of work before. Doctors have been able to change people's bodies and faces for many years, of course. They can rebuild a destroyed nose with skin from above the eyes. They can take teeth from one person and use them in the mouth of another. And they can even use bits of an animal's body to mend the body of a man. But until now, no one has tried to change one type of animal into another type of animal.

'The people on this island were built in my laboratory. Their animal bodies were cut and pushed into new shapes. But the changes to the body were only the start. I shaped their minds too. I changed their blood. They feel differently, think differently. They have even learnt to talk.'

'But why?!' I said. 'Why do you turn them into people, not into sheep, or horses, or ...?' It seemed a dangerous idea to choose the shape of man. Some things should be the business of religion, not science.

'Oh, I haven't only made people. Once or twice I've ...' He was silent, for a minute perhaps. 'How quickly the years pass!'

'But what is the purpose of your experiments? You hurt these animals terribly, but your science has no useful result.'

'Pain is just a little thing, Prendick. While you worry about pain, you are no better than an animal. Each of my experiments gives the answer to a question, a big question. But it also asks a new question. There is always more to find out.

'I came here with Montgomery eleven years ago. We had three boys with us from another Pacific island. They built the house for Montgomery and me. For themselves, they built the huts where the animal-people now live.

'My first experiments here were on sheep, but they weren't very successful. Sheep are too fearful, too stupid. Then I tried an ape. When my work was finished, this ape looked like a real man. He had no memory of his earlier life. I became his teacher, and after three or four months he could speak quite good English. He wasn't very clever, but I've known stupider men. I introduced him to the three boys. At first they were very afraid of him, but they soon started to like him more. He lived with them and copied their way of life. He built a hut like theirs. They even taught him to read.

'I was very pleased with my first ape-man. I planned to write a description of the experiment for a science magazine. But one day I visited him and he was making ape noises from the top of a tree. And he was never quite the same after that. The animal in him grew stronger and stronger. I decided to make a more successful animal-person before I told the scientific world about my work.

'For the last ten years, I have made more and more successful animal-people. The hands and feet are difficult, and none of them can smile. But the main problem is that the animal in them has always grown back. I haven't told the world about these small successes yet, because I can do better. I *will* do better. This puma ...'

He stopped himself suddenly. 'And that's the end of the story. The three boys are all dead now. There are a lot of accidents on this island. But Montgomery is still with me and …'

He stopped. I sat in silence, watching his face.

'How many are there?' I asked him finally.

'More than sixty, I think. I've made about one hundred and twenty in total, but many have died. There are a few women and they sometimes have children – but the children always die.'

'And when you've made these monsters, you send them to the huts,' I said.

'They choose to go there,' he explained. 'Most of them stay away from this place – a weak memory of their pain here, I think. And they follow the rules that the boys taught them. They call it the Law.

'So what do you think of me now?' he continued. 'Are you still afraid of me?'

To answer his question, I gave him back the guns.

'Keep them,' he said. He stood up and smiled. 'I'm glad everything's clear now. But you've had two busy days. You should get some rest. Goodnight.'

Chapter 10   The Taste of Blood

When I woke the next morning, Moreau was already busy in the laboratory. Montgomery and I escaped the puma's cries and went for a walk around the island. We soon met the ape-man and one of the pig-men.

'We greet you, Other-with-a-gun,' they said to Montgomery.

'There's a Third-with-a-gun now,' Montgomery said, 'so don't do anything stupid.'

The pig-man looked at me. 'The Third-with-a-gun, the Walker-with-tears-in-the-sea, has a thin white face,' he said.

'He has a thin black gun too,' said Montgomery.

'Yesterday he was crying and losing blood. You and the Master never cry. You never lose blood,' said the ape-man.

'You'll cry and lose blood soon if you're not careful,' Montgomery replied. 'Come on, Prendick.' He took my arm and we walked away.

The pig-man and ape-man stood watching us. 'Men speak, but this one says nothing,' said the pig-man.

'Yesterday he asked me about things to eat,' said his friend. 'He didn't know.'

I did not hear the rest of their conversation, but they were laughing.

Later we saw a dead rabbit, half eaten and without its head.

'Damn!' said Montgomery. 'What can this mean?' He looked carefully at the rabbit's body.

'I saw something like it on my first day here,' I said.

'Really? On your first day?' he asked.

'Yes. And I think I know the killer too. I can't be sure. But just before I found the rabbit, I saw one of your monsters by a stream. It was drinking like an animal, without its hands.'

'"Don't drink without cups. That is the Law. Are we not men?"' said Montgomery with a worried laugh. 'As soon as they're alone, they forget about the Law. And it's worst in the evening. They're most like animals when it's getting dark.' He stopped to think. 'But that's interesting,' he continued. 'Meat-eaters always like a drink after a kill. It's the taste of blood, you see – salty.'

'Well, the thing at the stream was the same monster that ran after me later on the beach.'

'Will you know him if you see him again?' asked Montgomery. He looked around us and checked his gun.

'I didn't see him very well, but I hit him hard with a stone. He'll probably still have some blood on his head.'

'I'm sure it was the leopard-man,' said Montgomery. 'Or perhaps one of the other big cats. But how can we prove that he killed the rabbit too? Damn rabbits! It was a big mistake to bring them here.'

I started to walk back to the house. Montgomery did not move.

'Let's go!' I called.

Finally he joined me. 'This is serious, Prendick,' he said. 'They mustn't learn to enjoy meat. If they do, well … we're all in trouble.'

Back at the house, Moreau agreed that the problem was very serious. That afternoon, the three of us and M'ling walked across the island to an open space near the animal-people's huts. Moreau took a little pipe from his pocket and put it to his mouth. It made a surprisingly loud noise. Soon the animal-people started to arrive: two of the pig-men first, then a big horse-person and a terrible bear-woman. When they saw Moreau, they dropped to the ground.

'His hands are the Hands that hurt.

'His hands are the Hands that make.

'His hands are the Hands that mend,' they said, throwing earth on their heads.

More and more animal-people were coming out of the trees, singly or in pairs, to join them in this strange activity.

'Sixty-two, sixty-three,' counted Moreau. 'There are four more.'

'I can't see my attacker,' I said.

Moreau made the noise with his pipe again. Finally, at the back of the crowd, I saw my attacker join the rest. There was a dark line of blood on his head.

'The leopard-man,' Montgomery said quietly in my ear.

'Stop!' said Moreau, in a loud, strong voice.

The animal-people sat on the ground and stopped talking.

'Where is the Sayer of the Law?' asked Moreau, and the hairy grey monster stood up.

'Say the words,' said Moreau.

The grey monster and the others began the words of the Law. When they reached 'Don't eat meat or fish. That is the Law,' Moreau held up his hand.

The grey monster and the others began the words of the Law.

'Stop!' he cried. The crowd was suddenly silent. They looked nervously at their neighbours, waiting for Moreau's next words.

'Someone has broken that Law,' he said.

'No one escapes,' said the Sayer of the Law.

'No one escapes,' repeated the rest of the crowd.

'Who was it?' asked Moreau, looking from face to face. The leopard-man looked worried, and some of the other big cats too.

Moreau stood in front of the leopard-man. 'Who was it?' he asked again in a terrible voice. 'If you break the Law ...' he said, turning to the crowd.

'... you go back to the House of Pain,' the crowd continued.

'The House of Pain, the House of Pain!' cried the ape-man in excitement.

Suddenly the leopard-man jumped at Moreau. Moreau fell back. The leopard-man ran away and the crowd followed. I followed with them, behind M'ling and Moreau. I found myself next to the bear-woman. 'No one escapes,' she laughed excitedly as we hurried through the trees.

We ran in the heat of the day for thirty minutes or more. Finally the leopard-man was in a corner of the island and could not escape us. But he was hiding.

We walked slowly towards the sea in a long line.

'Careful!' cried Montgomery. 'He'll move suddenly when we find him.'

'Back to the House of Pain, the House of Pain, the House of Pain,' sang the ape-man.

Suddenly I saw a pair of green eyes shining out from under the plants. It was the leopard-man! I will never forget the fear in those eyes. He already knew the pain that waited for him in Moreau's laboratory.

It was kinder to kill him quickly. I got out my gun and shot him between the eyes. He fell to the ground, dead.

In the same second, two of the other big cats jumped at him and bit deeply into his neck. Other faces came towards us.

'Don't kill him!' cried Moreau. Then he saw that it was too late. 'Damn it, Prendick!' he said. 'I wanted him in the laboratory!'

We pulled the meat-eaters away from the body. Then I walked away from the crowd.

I watched them take the body into the sea. All the animal-people still seemed very excited. I suddenly felt sick as I thought about the sad lives of these monsters. The problem was not only their pain in Moreau's laboratory. They then spent every day of their lives fighting against the animal in them. It was an impossible fight. In secret, they all broke the Law in their different ways. And the fear of the House of Pain never left them.

Chapter 11   The Puma Escapes

For the next two months, I lived quietly on the island. My dislike of Moreau and his work grew stronger. But soon the strange animal-people did not seem unusual to me.

I watched Montgomery and M'ling together with interest. M'ling was probably the most successful of Moreau's experiments. He was made from a bear, but he had bits of dog and horse in him too. He was not as clever as the ape-man, but he followed orders much better and looked more like a man. He lived in a small hut at the back of our house, not with the other animal-people in their huts. He followed Montgomery like a dog and most of the time Montgomery enjoyed his company. When Montgomery spoke kindly to him, he jumped around happily like an excited child. But after a few whiskies, Montgomery sometimes kicked him or threw stones at him. Even then, M'ling was happy to be at his master's side.

Montgomery and I did not become close friends. After his long time away from ordinary people, he was too strange. He seemed more comfortable with the animal–people than with me. And I stayed away from the animal–people as much as possible.

I dreamed day and night of ways to escape the island. I spent many hours on the beach, looking for ships. But they never came. And then something terrible happened that changed everything.

I woke at six one morning, had breakfast and went outside. Moreau walked past me and said a quick hello. Then he opened the door to his laboratory and went in. After many weeks on the island, I almost did not notice as the cries of the poor puma began for another day.

Then I heard a crash inside the laboratory. Suddenly something was running towards me – not a man, not an animal, but a monster. It had no skin, no face, but terrible yellow eyes, and drops of blood were coming from all over its body. It jumped at me. I held up my arm to protect myself. The monster crashed into me and I fell to the ground. As it ran towards the forest, I tried to get up. But there was a terrible pain in my arm and I could not move. I saw Moreau with blood on his face and a gun in his hand. He looked at me for a second, then followed the monster into the trees.

Finally I stood up. Montgomery arrived.

'The puma!' I cried. 'I was standing near the door, and …' I was silenced by the pain in my arm.

Montgomery had a look at it. 'Well, it's broken,' he said, 'and there's a lot of blood. But it isn't too serious. You'll live. Now, what were you saying about the puma?'

He cleaned my arm as I told him my story.

'Well, there's no sign of them now,' he said. 'I should go and help Moreau. That puma was strong.'

He gave me a gun and walked into the forest. Still in great pain, I went inside. I kept the door open and held the gun in my good hand.

The morning was as calm as death. There was no wind. The

sea was like a mirror. I kept my eyes on the place where I last saw Moreau and Montgomery. Where were they now?

I once heard Montgomery shouting 'Moreau! Moreau!' Then nothing. After many hours, I heard a gun shot far away in the forest. A long silence, then another shot. A shout, closer this time. Then silence again. Suddenly, a shot, very near. I looked round the corner and Montgomery was there. There were bits of grass in his hair and there were holes in the knees of his trousers. He looked hot and tired, and very worried. Behind him stood M'ling with a strange brown colour around his mouth. Was that blood?

'Has he come?' cried Montgomery.

'Moreau?' I asked. 'No.'

'Go back inside,' he continued. 'They're all crazy. Crazy! What's happening to them? I need some whisky.'

We went inside, leaving M'ling by the door. After a glass of whisky, Montgomery told me about his morning.

'We've seen no sign of Moreau or the puma. But the animal-people have gone crazy. We met two of the pig-men, and they had blood on their mouths. One of them attacked me. I don't understand it. No one's ever done that before − not even the meat-eaters! Well, I shot one of the pig-men in the head, and M'ling got the other with a bite in the neck. M'ling's damn teeth − probably saved my life today. We met a meat-eater too − one of the big cats − with blood on its mouth and a broken foot. I shot it. Well, it's better to be safe …'

'What does it all mean?' I asked.

Montgomery shook his head and picked up the whisky bottle.

I left him with his drink for some time. But he was clearly getting drunk, and that was dangerous on a day like this.

'Listen, Montgomery, something's happened to Moreau,' I said. 'He's been out for too long. We need to find him.'

Montgomery did not want to go. But in the end he agreed. We had a quick lunch, then stepped out into the heat of the day.

Chapter 12   The Search for Moreau

M'ling went in front. Montgomery followed, with his head down and his hands in his pockets. He could not walk in a straight line because of the whisky. My left arm was tied up and painful, but luckily my right arm was fine. I carried our only gun.

We took a narrow path through the trees. Suddenly M'ling stopped, listening. We listened too. Some animal-people were coming towards us.

'He's dead,' said one voice.

'He isn't dead, he isn't dead,' said another.

'We saw, we saw,' said some others.

There was a few seconds silence, then some crashes in the trees. Finally we saw six faces: the ape-man, the hairy grey Sayer of the Law, and four horse-men.

'What did you say?' asked Montgomery angrily. 'Where's the Master?'

They all looked at their friends. No one spoke. Finally the hairy Sayer of the Law said, 'He's dead. They saw.'

'Where is he?' continued Montgomery.

The hairy grey thing pointed away to our left.

'Is there a Law now?' asked the ape-man. 'Is it still "Don't do this and don't do that"? Is he really dead?'

'Is there a Law?' repeated his friends.

'Is there a Law, Other-with-a-gun? He is dead,' said the Sayer of the Law. They all stood watching us.

Montgomery's eyes were still swimming in whisky. 'Prendick,' he said, 'he's clearly dead, so ...'

I thought quickly and stepped towards the animal-men. 'Children of the Law,' I said loudly, 'he is *not* dead.' M'ling turned his sharp eyes on me, but I continued. 'He has changed his shape ... He has changed his body. For some time you won't see him.

He is … there,' I pointed up to the sky. 'You can't see him, but he can see you. Fear the Law.'

They looked unsure. 'He is great. He is good,' said the ape-man finally, looking fearfully up at the sky.

'And the other thing?' I asked them.

'The Thing-with-blood-and-screams is dead too,' said the Sayer of the Law.

'Good,' said Montgomery to himself.

'The Other-with-the-gun …' began the Sayer of the Law.

'Yes?' I said.

'He says the Master is dead.'

Montgomery was not too drunk to understand my purpose in all this. 'He's not dead,' he said now. 'He's no more dead than I am.'

'Some have broken the Law,' I continued. 'They will die. Some have died already. Show us the Master's old body.'

'It is this way, Walker-with-tears-in-the-sea,' said the Sayer of the Law.

We were following him through the trees when suddenly a rabbit crossed our path. Behind it came a great bear-man, too fast to stop. The Sayer of the Law stepped out of this monster's way. M'ling jumped at it but was pushed off. Montgomery turned to run. Quickly, I pulled out my gun and shot straight into the monster's ugly face. Its face was destroyed, but still it came towards us. It caught Montgomery in its arms as it fell to the ground – dead.

Slowly, Montgomery shook himself out of the monster's lifeless arms. The Sayer of the Law came nervously to look.

'You see,' I said to him. 'The Law is alive. This man is d because of the Law. No one escapes.'

'No one escapes,' he repeated.

His friends joined him to look at the dead bear-man.

Finally we continued our walk. At the west corr

island, we found the dead puma. It was shot in the shoulder, and half-eaten too. Then, a few metres away, we found another body. It lay face down, its white hair covered in blood.

With the animal-men's help, we carried Moreau's body slowly back to the house. It was getting dark. We heard many strange noises through the trees but we were not attacked again.

M'ling went off with the other animal-men. Montgomery and I could finally talk.

'We have to plan our escape from the island,' I said.

Montgomery was not drunk now, but his mind was very troubled. Life on the island without Moreau was impossible for him to imagine. 'No one wants me in the real world,' he said. 'It's OK for you, Prendick. But this place is the only home that I have. And what about the animal-people? The good ones? They need our protection.'

'What will happen to them if we go?' I asked.

'The meat-eaters will eat the others. They all change back to animals in the end.' He reached for the bottle of whisky and drank a large glass of it. He offered some to me, but I refused. Another glass disappeared down his neck, then another, as he talked about the animal-people.

'M'ling is the only person in the world who has really loved me,' he said drunkenly. 'Where's M'ling? Where is he? I want to have a drink with him. M'ling! M'ling!'

I tried to stop him. 'You can't give him drink. He'll …'

'Get out of my way!' shouted Montgomery. Suddenly his gun was pointing at me. I stepped back. 'Everything's gone wrong,' he said. 'Tomorrow I'll probably kill myself. But tonight I'm going ave some fun. I'm going to have a party.'

Chapter 13   Montgomery's Party

Montgomery turned and went out into the moonlight. 'M'ling! M'ling, old friend!' he shouted.

He found three animal-men on the beach and gave them all a drink. M'ling soon joined them. 'Drink and sing!' Montgomery was shouting. 'Let's have a party!'

The noise of this strange party was loud at first. It got slowly quieter as it moved along the beach. Finally, there was silence. I stood in the moonlight for a few minutes at the door to my room. Then I started to prepare for my escape the next day.

I made a pile in the garden of everything that I needed for the boat: food, clothes, some sheets for sails, containers for water, and much more. A few hours before morning, Montgomery's group returned. They were singing noisily on the beach, and breaking wood for some reason. But I was busy, working by the light of my oil lamp. I soon stopped noticing their noise.

When it was getting light, Montgomery's group finally stopped singing. There was a shout of 'More! More!' Some angry words followed, then a loud scream. The scream worried me. I stood and listened. There were more shouts. Then, suddenly, a gun shot sounded.

I picked up my own gun and hurried towards the noise. As I ran, I kicked some of the things in my pile. There was a crash of broken glass, but I did not stop. Who had the gun, and why were they shooting?

I opened the door and saw a small fire on the beach. Around it was a pile of bodies, fighting. Montgomery was calling my name. I ran towards the fire. I shouted as loudly as possible and shot into the air with my gun.

Someone cried, 'The Master! The Master!' The group stopped fighting. A number of animal-people ran away in fear and disappeared into the trees. I then turned to the bodies still by the fire.

Montgomery lay on his back with the hairy grey Sayer of the Law on top of him. The hairy monster was dead, but still held Montgomery's neck in its sharp teeth. M'ling lay next to them, with a big bite in his neck and a broken whisky bottle in his hand. Two other bodies lay near the fire. One did not move. The other was crying in pain. It sometimes lifted its head slowly, then dropped it again.

I pulled the Sayer of the Law off Montgomery — not an easy job, with my broken arm. Montgomery looked terrible, but still alive. I put a few drops of sea-water on his face, took off his jacket and rested his head on it. M'ling and the person next to him were dead. The last one's body was badly burnt in the fire, and after a few minutes he was dead too.

I knew very little about medicine. What could I do to help Montgomery? Before I could do anything, I heard a strange noise behind me. I looked around. Fire and clouds of black smoke were coming from the house! I thought back. The crash ... the broken glass. I knew immediately the reason for the fire. The broken glass was my oil lamp!

The fire was already burning strongly. It was impossible to save any of the things inside. My mind turned to my plan of escape, and I looked for the two boats on the beach. They were not there! Slowly, I understood. Montgomery's fire used wood. The wood of the two boats. The two boats that were my only hope of escape from this island.

I was so angry that I almost killed Montgomery with my gun. Then his hand moved, and he looked so weak. I could not hurt him. He shook with pain and opened his eyes for a minute. I lifted his head up a little. His eyes met mine.

'I'm sorry,' he said. 'The boats ... I've been so stupid ...'

His eyes closed and his head fell to one side. 'Montgomery?' I .'Montgomery!'

felt his heart. He was dead.

'I'm sorry,' he said. 'The boats … I've been so stupid …'

I sat alone on the beach for about an hour, doing nothing. Ideas raced through my head, but no sensible plan came to me.

Then three animal-men came out of the trees. Slowly they walked towards me. The smell of the dead bodies pulled them closer and closer.

Alone I faced them, with the gun in my one good hand. 'Get down on your knees!' I said loudly.

They stopped and looked at me. I repeated my words and moved towards them. One went down on his knees, then the other two.

I walked past the dead bodies, keeping my eyes on the three on their knees. 'They broke the Law,' I said, putting my foot on the Sayer of the Law. 'And now they are dead. Even the Sayer of the Law. Even the Other-with-the-gun. The Law is great.'

'No one escapes,' said one of the men on the ground.

'No one escapes,' I repeated. 'You must follow my orders. Now, stand up.'

They stood. I took Montgomery's gun from him, then said, 'Take him. Carry him out to the sea.'

They were afraid to touch Montgomery. But they were more afraid of my gun. Finally, they lifted up his body and walked into the sea with it. They did the same with the other bodies, then I sent them away. I needed some time to think. How could I live on the island now? How could I escape? The house was destroyed, so I could not even sleep without fear of attack.

The animal-people's fear of my gun was my only hope. I needed to become their master, a new Dr Moreau. After a short rest, I started walking towards their huts.

When I got there, I was hungry, thirsty and very tired. As bravely as I could, I walked towards a small group of the animal-people. They did not get down on their knees. I was too weak to order it. I just asked politely for food and drink, and they pointed towards one of the huts.

I was stupid. In that minute I lost my position as their master. They were never afraid of me as they were of Moreau.

In an empty hut, I ate some fruit. Then, with my gun in my hand, I fell into a troubled sleep.

When I woke up it was dark outside. My arm was hurting. At first I could not remember where I was. Then the terrible memories of the last two days came back to me.

I heard something in the hut. I saw a dark shadow near my legs. It was slowly moving. Who or what was it? I waited. Suddenly, something soft, warm and wet passed over my hand.

Chapter 14   Alone with the Animal-men

I almost screamed. 'Who's that?' I asked.

'*I*, Master,' said the shadow.

'Who are you?'

'They say that there is no Master now. But I know, I know. I carried the bodies into the waves for you, Walker-with-tears-in-the-sea. I carried the bodies of the people that you killed. I am yours, Master.'

I remembered him on the beach. A dog-man. He seemed safe.

'Good … that's good,' I said. His tongue passed over my hand again. 'But where are the others?'

'They are saying bad things. They are saying, "The Master is dead. The Other-with-a-gun is dead. The Walker-with-tears-in-the-sea is like us. We love the Law, and we will keep it. But we have no Master now, no House of Pain." They say these things. But they are wrong. I know.'

In the darkness, I reached for the dog-man's head and touched it lightly.

'Soon you will kill them all,' he continued.

'If they break the Law, I will come for them.'

'Master always knows best,' said my new friend.

We left the hut and found a crowd of animal-men around a fire.

'He is dead, the Master is dead,' said the ape-man. 'There is no House of Pain.'

'He is *not* dead,' I said in a loud voice. 'Even now He is watching us. The House of Pain has gone. But it will come again. And the Master too will come again. Every minute of every day, He is watching you and listening. There will be pain and death for anyone who breaks the Law.'

'True! True!' said the dog-man.

They were very surprised by my words. Animals can be clever, and dangerous. But only a real man can lie.

'The Walker-with-tears-in-the-sea says a strange thing,' said one of them.

'Can it be true?' said another.

For an hour we talked, and by the end many believed me. Finally, they went to their beds, and I went with them. I was safer with a group of them than with one alone.

This was the first night of ten months alone with the animal-men. In the first month, I spent a lot of time with them. I even started to like some of them – the dog-man and a few others. But as the months passed, the animal-people began to change. It became difficult for them to walk on two legs. Their hands became useless. Their bodies grew more and more hairy and they stopped wearing clothes. Their language skills suffered too. Their words became difficult to understand. Then they stopped using words completely. After about six months, the Law was almost completely forgotten. They still ate only fruit, but for the meat-eaters this could surely not last long.

Every day I watched the sea for ships. Three times I saw a sail and lit a fire. But no ship came close to the island. After many months, I decided to build my own boat. But, stupidly, I built it in the forest, far from the sea. It was destroyed as I pulled it over rough ground to the beach.

Then life got worse. As I was walking in the forest, I saw something red. A dead body. The body of my friendly dog-man.

The meat-eaters were back.

No one was living in the huts now. Most of the animal-people were sleeping by day, some in trees, some in holes, following their natural ways. At night they were awake, and their growls and screams filled the darkness. The dog-man's was the first of many dead bodies that I found around the island.

I too started to sleep by day. That way I could defend myself more easily from a night attack. I also started to build another boat, this time on the beach. When it was finished, it was stronger than the last one. But I had one problem that I could not solve. I needed fresh water for the journey that I was planning. But I had no container. I walked around the island again and again, looking for a possible container. But I found nothing.

Then a happy day arrived. There was a little sail out at sea, and it was coming closer! I lit a fire and fed it all day. The sail came towards the island, slowly, slowly. When night fell, it was still a long way from land. All night I kept my fire bright. In the light of the fire I saw many eyes watching me. But the animal-men could not make their own fires now, and were afraid of mine.

In the morning the sail was much nearer. I could see two men in a little boat. They were sitting low down in it, one at each end. When they were very close, I started shouting. I waved my jacket. But the men did not notice me.

Suddenly, a great white bird flew up out of the boat. Again, the men did not move. A cold fear took hold of me.

Finally, the boat reached the beach. The men, long dead, fell to pieces when I pulled them out of the boat. One had bright red hair. The other had a hat with the word *Ipecacuanha* on it.

Three of the meat-eaters were soon by my side, interested in the smell of the bodies. I was too weak to keep them away. But I could not watch their terrible meal. I pulled the boat into the water and sailed it along the beach.

That night I slept in the boat. In the morning I filled its water container at the stream. Then I shot and cooked three rabbits and picked a large amount of fruit. I put the food and drink into the boat and sailed away from the island.

The wind took me slowly southwest, and soon the blue of the ocean was all around me. After the last few months, it felt good to be completely alone.

Three days later I was picked up by a ship. I seemed crazy to the sailors, of course. I was wearing almost nothing. It was many months since my last conversation with a real person. And my description of the island and its strange population was difficult to believe.

◆

For thirty years I have kept quiet about my adventures on the island. Perhaps even now no one will believe me. But what does it matter? I am an old man. I will soon be dead.

I have lived a quiet life since my return from the Pacific. People do not feel comfortable in my company. They see something strange in me. Perhaps I became a little like the animal-people who I lived with for all those months. And I do not feel comfortable in the company of others, either. I fear that secretly they are animal-people. I fear that the animal in them will soon grow stronger. I fear that one day they will attack. It is a fear that never completely leaves me.

ACTIVITIES

Chapters 1–2

Before you read

1 You are going to read a story by H. G. Wells. He also wrote *The War of the Worlds* and *The Invisible Man*. Have you read these stories, or seen films of them? What do you know about them?

2 Look at the Word List at the back of the book. Check the meaning of new words, then talk to another student.

   a Which words on the list are words for animals?

   b What is your opinion of scientists who use animals in their laboratories?

3 At the start of the story, Prendick is in a small boat in the middle of the ocean with two other men. Only Prendick stays alive. What happens to the others, do you think?

While you read

4 Are these sentences right (✓) or wrong (✗)?

   a The sailor throws himself into the sea when
      he gets the shortest stick.   .....

   b Montgomery nurses Prendick back to health.   .....

   c The sailors like M'ling.   .....

   d Captain Davis is usually drunk.   .....

   e Prendick is paying Davis to take him to land.   .....

After you read

5 Why are these ships important to the story?

   a the *Lady Vain*

   b the *Ipecacuanha*

6 Who or what fits this description?

   a very ugly

   b too big for its cage

   c red-haired

7 What do we know about Montgomery?

Chapters 3–4

Before you read

8 Discuss these questions.

    a Have you ever done an experiment on an animal in biology? Describe it.

    b Are there any types of scientific experiment that no one should do?

9 What kinds of people and animals live on an island in the middle of the South Pacific, do you think?

While you read

10 Put these sentences in the right order. Number them 1–5.

    a Montgomery opens the rabbits' cages. .....

    b Prendick sees M'ling's ear. .....

    c Montgomery's master says that Prendick can't come to their island. .....

    d Montgomery's master helps Prendick to land. .....

    e Davis's sailors throw Prendick into the boat from the *Lady Vain*. .....

After you read

11 Answer these questions.

    a Why does Montgomery want rabbits on the island?

    b What does Prendick know about Moreau's old life in Britain?

    c What do we know about M'ling? Why does he look so strange, do you think?

12 Work with another student. Act out a conversation between Prendick and Captain Davis.

    Student A: You are Captain Davis. Tell Prendick that he has to leave the ship. Explain the reasons for this. You are not going to change your mind.

    Student B: You are Prendick. You want to stay on the ship. You don't want to go back into the *Lady Vain*'s little boat. Ask the captain to change his mind.

Chapters 5–6

Before you read

13 Discuss these questions. What do you think?

    a Why do Moreau and Montgomery keep the inside door to Prendick's room locked, do you think?

    b Can you guess the type of biology that Moreau is doing on the island?

While you read

14 Complete the sentences with 'Prendick' or a type of animal.

    a Prendick goes for a walk to escape the noise of the …………………….. .

    b There is a dead …………………….. near the stream.

    c There is a group of people in the forest that look like …………………….. .

    d Something attacks …………………….. on the beach.

    e …………………….. hides from Montgomery in the shadows of the trees.

After you read

15 Answer these questions.

    a What is strange about the person that Prendick sees at the stream?

    b Why does Prendick run away from Montgomery?

16 Discuss this question. What problems will Prendick have if he lives without help from Moreau and Montgomery?

17 Work with another student. Act out a conversation between Prendick and Montgomery.

    Student A: You are Prendick. Describe your evening walk in the forest and the attack on the beach. Try to find out more from Montgomery about the strange people on the island.

    Student B: You are Montgomery. You want to be kind to Prendick, but you don't want to answer his questions.

Chapters 7–8

Before you read

18 Discuss these questions.

    a In these chapters, Prendick meets more people on the island. Will they be dangerous?

    b What will happen when Moreau and Montgomery find Prendick?

While you read

19 Who is it? Choose the correct name.

Prendick   Montgomery   the ape-man
the Sayer of the Law (x 2)

    a His arms hang below his knees. ....

    b He is covered in grey hair. ....

    c He has three fingers on each hand. ....

    d He points a gun at Prendick. ....

    e He walks into the sea. ....

After you read

20 Work with another student.

    a Describe the place where the animal-people live.

    b The ape-man calls Prendick a 'five-man'. What does he mean?

    c In your own words, list five rules that are part of the animal-people's Law. *They can't …*

    d Prendick tries to kill himself. Why? And why does he stop before it is too late?

    e Do you think that Moreau's words to Prendick on the beach are true? Give reasons for your answer.

    f Chapter 8 ends with the words, '… in that minute they had the look of small children. Small children who were trying to think.' What are they thinking? Why are their thoughts dangerous?

Chapters 9–10

Before you read

21 Discuss these questions.

    a Moreau says that he makes the animal-people from ordinary animals. What do you think about this kind of scientific work?

    b Someone dies at the end of Chapter 10. Who, do you think?

While you read

22 Are these sentences right (✓) or wrong (✗)?

    a The animal-people look like people, but they think like animals.   .....

    b The animal-people built Moreau's house.   .....

    c The best animal-people were made from sheep.   .....

    d Moreau's first ape-man could read.   .....

    e The three boys were all killed in accidents.   .....

    f Moreau wrote the Law for the animal-people.   .....

    g The pig-man and ape-man don't think Prendick is like Moreau and Montgomery.   .....

    h The leopard-man jumps at Moreau.   .....

    I Prendick shoots the leopard-man.   .....

    j Moreau wants to experiment on the leopard-man's dead body.   .....

After you read

23 Discuss these questions.

    a Why does Moreau make the animal-people?

    b Why does he keep his work secret from other scientists?

    c What do the animal-people think about Prendick? Are they afraid of him as they are afraid of Moreau?

    d Why does Prendick shoot the leopard-man?

    e What does Prendick think of Moreau's experiments now?

Chapters 11–12

Before you read

24 Discuss these questions.

    a In Chapter 11, Prendick writes, 'And then something terrible happened that changed everything.' What happens, do you think?

    b Who will act more sensibly in a dangerous position – Montgomery or Prendick?

While you read

25 Who is it? Complete two sentences with each name.

    M'ling   Prendick   The puma   Montgomery

    a .... is happy when he's with Montgomery.

    b .... has no skin.

    c .... breaks Prendick's arm.

    d .... kills a pig-man with his teeth.

    e .... drinks too much whisky.

    f .... lies to the animal-men about Moreau.

    g .... shoots a bear-man that is running after a rabbit.

    h .... is worried about the safety of the animal-people.

After you read

26 Who or what are they?

    a the Other-with-the-gun

    b the Walker-with-tears-in-the-sea

    c the Thing-with-blood-and-screams

27 Why:

    a does Prendick tell the animal-men that Moreau is not dead?

    b does Montgomery not want to leave the island?

Chapters 13–14

Before you read

28 How does the story end, do you think? Discuss these questions with another student.

    a Will Montgomery and Prendick leave the island? How?

    b What will happen to the animal-people?

While you read

29 Put these sentences in the right order. Number them 1–9.

    a Four people die on the beach.   .....

    b Prendick prepares to leave the island in one of the little boats.   .....

    c Prendick makes friends with a dog-man.   .....

    d A boat arrives on the island.   .....

    e The dog-man is killed.   .....

    f Montgomery dies.   .....

    g The house is destroyed in a fire.   .....

    h Prendick reaches a safe place.   .....

    I Montgomery starts a party with some animal-men on the beach.   ......

After you read

30 List the changes that Prendick notices in the animal-men. There are eight changes in total.

31 Work with another student. Act out a conversation between Prendick and one of the sailors on the ship that saves him.

    Student A: You are Prendick. Talk about the island and the animal-men.

    Student B: You are a sailor. You don't believe Prendick. Tell him your reasons.

Writing

32 You are Moreau. Choose an important day on the island and write about it in your notebook.

33 You are Montgomery, living on the island before Prendick's arrival. Describe your life and the way that you feel about Moreau and the animal-people.

34 You work for a newspaper. Write a report about the life, work and death of Dr Moreau. (You have read Prendick's story and the newspapers from the time before Moreau left England.)

35 You are Prendick. Decide how long you have been on the island. Write a message asking for help. You are going to put your message in a bottle and throw it into the sea.

36 You are Captain Davis. Write about the days that Prendick is on board the *Ipecacuanha* for the ship's records.

37 Some of the animal-people are talking about something important that happened in the story. Write their conversation.

38 You are Prendick. Write a letter to the family of Captain Davis of the *Ipecacuanha* to tell them about his death. Give some information about the last year of his life – but be polite.

39 You are the sailor on the little boat with Captain Davis. You have been lost at sea for many days, and you will soon be dead. Write a letter to your family to say goodbye. Tell them why you are not on board the *Ipecacuanha* now. Describe your days on the little boat.

40 You are the captain of a ship that visits the island five years after the deaths of Moreau and Montgomery. Describe the island and the animals that live there.

41 You are the master of an island, ship, school or workplace. Write a 'Law' – a list of rules that people must follow.

WORD LIST

ape (n) an animal that is a close relative of man

bear (n) a large, strong animal; bears can be white, brown or black

biology (n) the scientific study of animals and plants

board (n) if you are **on board**, you are on a ship or boat

cage (n) a place for keeping animals or birds behind metal bars

captain (n) the boss of a ship

container (n) something that you can keep things in, for example a box or bottle

damn (adj/v) a word that a very angry person uses

drunk (adj) acting differently after too much wine or beer, for example. If you speak **drunkenly**, your words are unclear or not sensible

experiment (n/v) a scientific test to discover something

growl (n/v) a deep, angry sound made by an animal

laboratory (n) a room where people do scientific tests

lamp (n) something that produces light from electricity, oil or gas

leopard (n) a large yellow and black animal of the cat family, from Africa and South Asia

master (n) a man who makes the rules for other people's lives

monster (n) an ugly or large animal that people fear in stories

puma (n) a large, brown animal of the cat family, from North and South America

rabbit (n) a small animal with long ears that lives underground

rule (n/v) the government of a country

whisky (n) a strong drink; a lot of whisky is produced in Scotland, for example